KIT CARS

629.2
En

Engen, Gavin M
   Kit cars; cars you can build your-
self. Lerner 1977
  51p illus
   629.2

.9964 795

KIT CARS

CARS YOU CAN BUILD YOURSELF

GAVIN M. ENGEN

Lerner Publications Company ▪ Minneapolis, Minnesota

ACKNOWLEDGMENTS: The illustrations are reproduced through the courtesy of: p. 29, A & A Fiberglass, Inc.; pp. 14, 15, 17, 26, Antique & Classic Cars, Inc.; pp. 6, 18, 19, Autokit Industries; pp. 28, 42, 43, Blakely Auto Works; p. 33, Domus; pp. 4, 12, Elegant Motors, Inc.; pp. 9, 10, 30, Elite Enterprises, Inc.; p. 40, Fiberfab, Inc.; pp. 20, 21, Karma Coachworks, Ltd.; pp. 27, 44, 45, 47, 48, 49, 50, 51, Kelmark Engineering, Inc.; pp. 24, 25, Mini Woodie Inc.; p. 38, Minnesota Auto Specialties; pp. 22, 23, Pegasus Design Corporation; pp. 34, 35, 36, 37, Perfect Plastics Industries, Inc.

LIBRARY OF CONGRESS CATALOGING IN PUBLICATION DATA

Engen, Gavin M.
    Kit Cars.

    (Superwheels and Thrill Sports)
    SUMMARY: A survey of available component car kits used to transform certain small car chassis into replicas of more elaborate cars.

    1. Automobiles, Home-built. [1. Automobiles — Bodies. 2. Handicraft] I. Title.

TL225.E59   629.2'6   77-6203
ISBN 0-8225-0417-0

Published simultaneously in Canada by J. M. Dent & Sons (Canada) Ltd., Don Mills, Ontario.

Manufactured in the United States of America.

International Standard Book Number: 0-8225-0417-0
Library of Congress Catalog Card Number: 77-6203

2 3 4 5 6 7 8 9 10 85 84 83 82 81 80 79

CONTENTS

INTRODUCTION

REPLICARS AND CLASSICS
Auburn 856 Speedster   13
1934 Frazer Nash   15
Alfa-Romeo 1931   16

EXOTICS
Invader GT5   19
Manx SR-2   20
March Hare   23

STOCK-BODIED CONVERSIONS
Mini Woodie   24
Elegance   29

VANS AND TRUCKS
Laser 49er Mini Van   31
Flatback   32

BUGGIES
Tuff Tub   35
Boss Bug   36

ROADSTERS
MAS 1923 "T" Roadster   39
Liberty SLR   41
Blakely Bearcat   42

STREET MACHINES
Sleeper   45
Reverie   46
Tory   48
Liberator   50

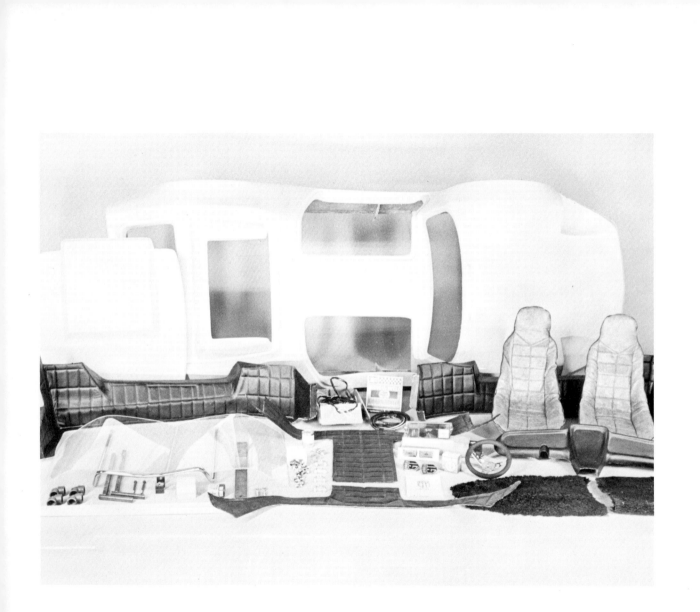

INTRODUCTION

What is the next best thing to owning an authentic classic car? Building a replica of one! With a component car kit, almost anyone can assemble a classic car—or any other type of vehicle—virtually by hand.

The term component, or "kit," car refers to a vehicle that is hand built from separate components, or parts. These parts are designed and manufactured by various auto specialty companies, and are packaged in kits. The consumer buys the kit directly from the manufacturer or dealer and then sets about assembling it. If the buyer does not want to construct the vehicle, however, the manufacturer often will do the job.

Most of the essential parts needed to build the vehicle are included in the kit, but not all. Generally, the parts that make up the car's body are supplied. The power train parts—chassis, engine, and transmission—must be provided by the builder. Over the years, builders have found the Volkswagen to be the most adaptable vehicle for kit car construction. Today, most kit cars are built around VW chasses, engines, and transmissions. For high-powered component models, V6 and V8 GT engines and transmissions are installed.

Not all component kits are alike. Some contain one-piece bodies, and others contain separate body pieces that must be welded or bolted onto pre-existing VW body parts. The builder does not need a lot of mechanical skill to build a kit car, but he or she does need some mechanical aptitude and the ability to follow instructions. Easy-to-understand instructions are included in every kit. Generally, only average garage tools are called for in assembling the vehicles.

Kit car companies manufacture a wide variety of vehicles. There are classic cars and replicars, exotic sports cars, vans and trucks, dune buggies, and roadsters, to name a few. And for every model, there is a wide variety of accessories to choose from. These accessories include air horns, decals, interior upholstery, air conditioning, chrome wheels, mag wheels, AM-FM stereo radio, and 8-track tape player.

A TYPICAL KIT CAR

By looking a little more closely at one of these cars, we can get a better idea of what a component car is and how it is constructed. The car that will be used for illustration is the Laser 917, a component sports car model that is manufactured by Elite Enterprises, Inc., of Cokato, Minnesota.

Laser 917. The Laser 917 is a fully engineered sports car kit. Over the years, the strength and durability of its component parts have been proven again and again. The photograph shows the kit's component parts. The one-piece body of the Laser 917 mounts on a full-length VW chassis and uses standard VW running gear, engine, transaxle, suspension, brakes, steering, and other parts. A Corvair or Porsche engine is optional.

Components Used. The Laser 917 will accommodate a chassis from any stock VW 2-door sedan, 1947-76, except a Super Beetle with MacPherson front suspension. The Laser body will also fit any Karmann Ghia chassis.

9

Specifications
   Length. . . . . 170"
   Width. . . . . 77"
   Height. . . . . 43½"
   Wheelbase. . . . . 94½"
Price of Vehicle. $4,295

No shortening of either the VW or Karmann Ghia chassis is necessary. The Laser will accommodate any VW engine, as well as Porsche 4-cylinder and Corvair engine. (An adaptor is required for Corvair engines.)

Construction. Construction of the vehicle requires simple hand tools and three to four weekends of time. The builder begins by removing the VW body from the chassis and relocating the shift lever. (1965 and older VWs require shock tower adaptors.) The body is then set on the chassis and bolted down. The steering column and master cylinder brake reservoir are installed, the wiring is connected to the steering column, and the bumpers are installed. Next, the wheels and tires are bolted on. After the upholstered seats are bolted to the VW floor pan and the steering wheel is installed, the car is ready to drive.

General Features. The Laser 917 is very responsive, with quick, solid handling. Its sleek design improves crosswind and high-speed handling characteristics. And its short turning radius provides steering agility. The addition of a Corvair or Porsche engine gives outstanding acceleration and top speed.

When completely assembled, kit cars are generally used as hobby vehicles for leisure-time activities. Some of the more functional vehicles, however, like the vans and trucks, are put to everyday use.

People who build kit cars find that it is a good hobby. But they also find that there are practical reasons for building kit cars. For one thing, it is economical. Buying and assembling a kit car is less expensive than buying a comparable car on the market. For another thing, kit car building offers an unusual opportunity for individual self-expression. Builders are free to create their own designs or alter existing designs. For these and other reasons, kit car construction is fast becoming a popular hobby among car enthusiasts.

REPLICARS & CLASSICS

AUBURN 856 SPEEDSTER

The sleek Auburn 856 Speedster is a replica of the famous Auburn speedster last produced in 1936. Its fiberglass body is similar to the smooth-flowing design of the original. Even the four chrome exhaust headers behind each front fender and the slanted hood panels have been reproduced.

The Auburn 856 Speedster can be constructed around any standard automobile chassis. Frames and engines made by Ford and GM are often used in the construction of the car. A V8/4-barrel engine is able to provide the needed acceleration power for the 3,300-pound vehicle. This beauty from the past also boasts automatic transmission, power steering, and power brakes. Best of all, the car is easy to service. Included as standard equipment in this magnificent automobile are cushion-ride front and rear coil springs, a leather interior, a coach-style convertible top, removable side windows or curtains, tilt-adjustable steering column, and deluxe radio.

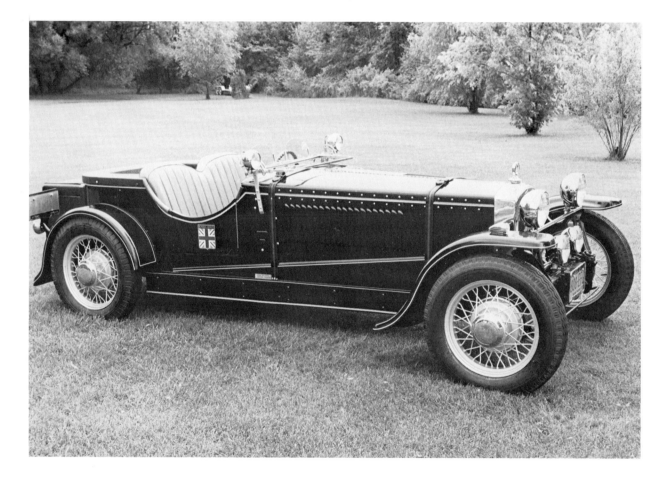

1934 FRAZER NASH

The smart-looking Frazer Nash is a practical, all-weather sports car. The car's body comes in a Frazer Nash replicar kit that can be mounted on any VW Bug chassis. Using average garage tools, a person can construct the basic car body in about 50 hours. Including overhauls, wiring, upholstery work, and clean-up, the process should take about 100 hours.

With its extended wheelbase, the Frazer Nash rides smoothly and handles well. The car also offers good weather protection (there is an easily attached canvas roof), a roomy interior, and storage space both behind the rear seat and under the hood. Other features include a windscreen and replaceable fenders and body components. The car retains the VW exhaust system along with heaters and temperature controls.

ALFA-ROMEO 1931

The Alfa-Romeo 1931 is a copy of one of the great racing cars of automotive history. The car is easy to build, requiring a total of 90 to 100 hours to complete. Only average garage tools are needed for assembly, although some welding would speed up the work.

The best feature of the Alfa-Romeo 1931 is its detailing; the rivets are molded in to give the car its authentic appearance. Another feature is the removable tail section for easy en-gine tune-up. The Alfa also has a wide variety of accessories to choose from. Among these items are a "Brooklands" style windscreen, wire wheel covers, and special hubcaps. One thing that the Alfa does not have is a top, but the car actually looks best without one.

When completed, the Alfa is much lighter than a standard VW and has added perform-ance. If the builder wishes, however, he or she can increase the engine power even further.

EXOTICS

INVADER GT5

A flashy car with many important features, the Invader GT5 is a popular automotive project for builders. The GT5 fiberglass body bolts directly to a VW chassis through the same holes the VW body was mounted with. Two different models of the Invader are available, and both have engine compartments that will accommodate VW, Porsche, Corvair, or Mazda engines.

Among the Invader's special features are its doors. The gull-wing doors provide easy entrance and exit for passengers, as well as excellent visibility. In warm weather they remove quickly and easily to convert the Invader GT5 into an open-air roadster. If the car is left in the sun, however, heat build-up through the plexiglass can be a problem. But once the car is driven again, the flow-through ventilation system in the doors provides enough air to eliminate the heat.

The GT5's aerodynamic wedge shape and front spoiler keep the car stable on the road. And the car's reduced weight and low center of gravity give it excellent handling ability. The Invader's reduced weight also means better mileage and less wear.

The Invader's dashboard features a walnut finish.

MANX SR-2

Any VW chassis from the years 1949 through 1975 can be used in the sporty Manx SR-2. Once the chassis is prepared, the SR-2 can be assembled in three days or less by an average person using ordinary hand tools. Besides the chassis, components used from the VW include engine, steering column, horn, gas tank, and battery. Everything else is furnished with the kit.

An interesting feature of the SR-2 is that its top and doors are filled with soundproofing material. There is also over 12 cubic feet of storage space in the car; storage space is provided both behind the seats and under the hood.

Because of its 80-inch wheelbase, the SR-2 is quick and responsive. The ride is firm, and the car accelerates and stops better than the stock VW. Also, steering response is quicker and fuel economy is improved.

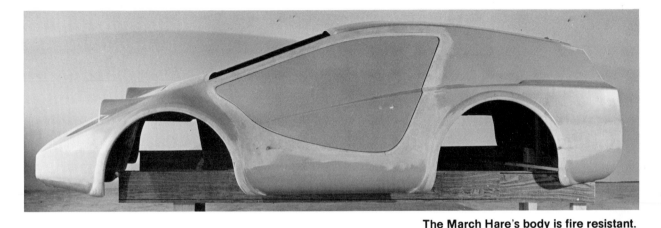

MARCH HARE

This truly exotic-looking car is a safe, functional vehicle that employs a simple and inexpensive power system. Constructed on a VW chassis (any year), the car incorporates many VW items, so extra hardware parts are easy to acquire.

The two-passenger March Hare measures 152 inches in length, 68 inches in width, and stands 46 inches high. After the chassis is shortened to standard dune buggy length, the wheelbase measures 80 inches. Average weight of the March Hare is 1,450 pounds.

With its VW chassis, the wedge-shaped March Hare is lighter, lower, wider, and more streamlined than the standard VW. This results in improvements in acceleration, top speed, braking, cornering, tire life, cross-wind stability, and gas mileage.

STOCK-BODIED CONVERSIONS

MINI WOODIE

The Mini Woodie was designed to capture the look of the wood-bodied station wagons of years past. No particular year's model has been copied here, however. This is so the builder can construct the car according to his or her own personal preferences.

The Mini Woodie fits any VW Bug sedan or convertible chassis and retains much of the VW body (engine, suspension, etc.). Using simple tools (except those required to remove the top of the VW), the builder can construct this car in approximately 30 to 40 hours.

The Mini Woodie drives and handles much the same as the stock VW. Other features, however, are improved. Headroom is increased by 2½ inches, and storage space is increased by 6 cubic feet. Vision is also greatly improved.

Mini Woodie (Stock Bodied Conversion)

Alfa-Romeo 1931 (Replicar-Classic)

Reverie (Street Machine)

Blakely Bearcat (Roadster)

ELEGANCE

For VW owners who love the economy and maneuverability of their Bugs but who still yearn for a classier car, the Elegance is the answer. In 10 hours you can bolt the Elegance kit onto your car without fiberglassing, welding, drilling, or cutting. What is more, no special skills or tools are required. (For any 1949-76 VW, Standard and Super Beetle.)

VANS & TRUCKS

LASER 49er MINI VAN

The Laser 49er is a completely new concept in mini sports vans. It represents a move away from the large, gas-gulping commercial cargo vans to the smaller economy van that can be used as a family vehicle or a small business van.

Two people can convert the Laser 49er Mini Van in one day. Start with any stock VW 2-door sedan chassis and install a VW, Porsche, or Corvair engine. From there, follow the carefully prepared instruction sheet to complete the conversion. Your van, when finished, will measure 173.5 inches long, 72 inches wide (100 inches with doors open), and 57 inches high (80 inches with doors open). These dimensions also provide 12 cubic feet of luggage space inside the rear hatch.

The Laser 49er is weather tight and rattle free, and it can accommodate five adults with room to spare. It has excellent visibility and maneuverability. And, as an added plus, it is a real eye stopper!

FLATBACK

The Flatback kit transforms any 1947-76 VW Beetle (except sunroof or convertible model) into either an economical pickup or a useful camper. Both models drive, park, and handle like the original car and get almost the same gas mileage. Both can be used for occasional hauling or as full-time delivery vehicles. And both have ample storage room. The camper sleeps two adults and has a locking rear window that provides excellent rear vision.

Construction of both the Flatback pickup and the Flatback camper is quite simple and can be completed in one weekend.

BUGGIES

TUFF TUB

A sturdy dune buggy, the four-passenger Tuff Tub recalls the classic styling of the Model "T" Ford. The Tub, however, is constructed around a VW chassis (any year) and houses a VW, Porsche, Corvair, or V6 engine.

Because the Tuff Tub body kit has been designed exclusively for the standard full-length Volkswagen chassis, no modifications are required. This makes installation fast and easy.

Once assembled and on the road, the Tuff Tub performs impressively. Steering is lighter and much quicker than in the standard VW, tire life is longer, acceleration is improved, and gas economy is increased.

BOSS BUG

Like the Tuff Tub, the Boss Bug is designed for ease of assembly. The kit is engineered for either the novice or the expert, and it provides easy-to-follow instructions and illustrations as well.

The four-passenger Boss Bug features a heavy-duty fiberglass body. The body will fit any year VW chassis that has been shortened to standard dune buggy length. The car will also accommodate a VW, Porsche, Corvair, or V6 engine.

Driving characteristics of the VW are improved with the Boss Bug kit. Acceleration and gas economy are better, steering is lighter and much quicker, tire life is extended, and braking performance is improved.

ROADSTERS

MAS 1923 "T" ROADSTER

This powerful-looking roadster is a departure from most of the kit car models shown in this book. Both the chassis and body are manufactured by MAS (Minnesota Auto Specialties), and they are designed to use components from any domestic or foreign car. Because there are no space restrictions, there is no limitation on the car's performance; any size engine is acceptable.

To construct the car, basic mechanical and bodyworking tools are needed. There is also a minimum of welding to do. The builder installs the engine, transmission, and other components of his or her choice. Color scheme and all interior and exterior furnishings depend on the builder's preference also.

The MAS roadster handles well due to good weight distribution and low total weight. And maintenance on the vehicle is simplified because all of the parts are in the open.

LIBERTY SLR

The Liberty SLR (super light roadster) is styled after a traditional European sports racer of the late Twenties. It is a basic, no-nonsense automobile that offers much in the way of driving excitement.

The kit is engineered primarily for ease of assembly. Even the novice car builder can be successful, for only a minimum of skill and experience are required of the builder, and only basic hand tools are needed for assembly. The car is also engineered to accommodate a small block Ford engine, transmission, and rear chassis. The most frequently used components are from Mustang, Cougar, Comet V8, or Falcon V8 vehicles.

BLAKELY BEARCAT

Comfort, durability, and quality construction best describe the Blakely Bearcat. The kit is based on Pinto components and comes with the body pre-assembled to the frame. Some welding is required, but that can be done in 15 minutes at a local welding shop.

The Bearcat includes such features as a roomy, lockable trunk, lockable doors, upholstered interior, sliding side windows, and a rollbar with cover. On the road, the car offers superior acceleration and handling, a soft, comfortable ride, and excellent gas mileage.

STREET MACHINES

SLEEPER

"Sleeper" is the perfect name for this kit model, for behind its mild Volkswagen exterior is the engine power to accelerate from 0 to 60 mph in 6 seconds, and to reach a top speed of 140 mph.

The Sleeper conversion kit includes a tubular steel chassis as well as most of the parts needed to mount a V8 engine with 4-speed or Olds Toronado automatic transmission. Any VW body can then be centered over the chassis and bolted down. To construct the Sleeper, the builder needs normal hand tools and average mechanical skill.

The two-passenger Sleeper weighs slightly more than the stock VW, but it offers good gas mileage and is very comfortable to drive.

The Sleeper carries V8 power in its back seat.

REVERIE

During the 1960s, the Chevy Corvair was one of the most popular cars in America because of its excellent handling and visibility, its parking ease, comfort, interior room, luggage space, and traction. But it had some drawbacks as well, most of which involved the power train.

Now, however, it is possible to overcome those drawbacks inexpensively and efficiently. With the Reverie V8-Vair Conversion Kit from Kelmark, it is easy to build a Corvair with a Chevy V8 engine. The car offers all the advantages of the original Corvair, plus the kind of handling and acceleration that you'd expect from an expensive sports car.

All that is needed is a 1965 or later Corvair, a Chevy V8 engine, a GM crossflow radiator, a few simple tools, and the Kelmark V8-Vair conversion kit. By paying careful attention to the instruction booklet, two people with average mechanical ability can produce a driveable V8-powered Corvair in a weekend.

TORY

The Tory Corvair conversion kit is another option for the Corvair enthusiast who wants a mid-engine automatic GT car. Like the Reverie, the Tory offers a simple, inexpensive way to enjoy the many good points of the Corvair and at the same time to overcome some of its original design problems.

In constructing the Tory, the most difficult step may be the first—finding a Corvair (1965 or later) that is in good condition. The

The Tory features Toronado power, plus four-passenger seating.

Tory kit provides the other necessary items to install an Olds Toronado engine and GM automatic transmission. The conversion requires no welding, no engine hoist, and no tools beyond normal hand tools and a floor jack. The drive train installs from beneath.

The Tory offers simple assembly, sports-car handling and power, and all the other features that once made the Corvair one of America's most popular cars.

LIBERATOR

The Liberator is a powerful street machine that features exotic Italian styling, quality production parts, and superior performance.

The streamlined fiberglass body comes pre-assembled from the factory, ready to mount on a tubular steel frame. Either a V6 or V8 engine with GM 4-speed or automatic transmission can be installed in the car. The suspension, engine, drive train components, and body accessories are easily obtainable, so repairs can be done at any reputable garage without long waits for parts.

The Liberator is designed with careful attention to details. It is available with power windows, air conditioning, and sound proofing. The car is not simply a show car, however. It is a quality automobile that combines looks and power for racing or everyday use.

Superwheels & Thrill Sports

AMERICAN RACE CAR DRIVERS
INTERNATIONAL RACE CAR DRIVERS
THE DAYTONA 500
THE INDIANAPOLIS 500
AIRPLANE RACING
DRAG RACING
ICE RACING
ROAD RACING
TRACK RACING

MOPED MANIA
MOTORCYCLE RACING
MOTORCYCLES ON THE MOVE
MOTOCROSS MOTORCYCLE RACING
GRAND NATIONAL CHAMPIONSHIP RACES
THE WORLD'S BIGGEST MOTORCYCLE RACE:
    THE DAYTONA 200
YESTERDAY'S MOTORCYCLES
BICYCLE ROAD RACING
BICYCLE TRACK RACING
BICYCLES ON PARADE
SNOWMOBILE RACING

SKYDIVING

AUTO BRIGHTWORK
CLASSIC SPORTS CARS
DINOSAUR CARS: LATE GREAT CARS
    FROM 1945 TO 1966
KIT CARS: CARS YOU CAN BUILD
    YOURSELF
HOME-BUILT AIRPLANES
VANS: THE PERSONALITY VEHICLES
YESTERDAY'S CARS
YESTERDAY'S FIRE ENGINES

Lerner Publications Company
241 First Avenue North, Minneapolis, Minnesota 55401